Book Description

Throughout sporting history, countless moments have left people worldwide with their jaws dropped. Countless moments that motivated the world and left people inspired by what they just witnessed. Countless moments of absolute magic and disbelief at the thought that such an achievement was possible. However, despite so many moments of sheer brilliance throughout sporting history, 20 stand out as being the *20 Greatest Sporting Moments of All Time.*

Moments such as Michael Jordan's "The Shot" versus the Cavaliers, the Federer versus Nadal 2008 Wimbledon final, Usain Bolt's masterclass at the 2008 Beijing Olympics, Michael Phelps bringing home eight golds from the 2008 Beijing Olympics, Super Bowl LI in 2017, Tiger Woods' return to golf's elite, The Rumble in the Jungle, Leicester City defying 5000/1 odds to win the English Premier League, and South Africa winning the 1995 Rugby World Cup. These are just some of the incredible sporting moments that make up this epic sporting catalog of the *20 Greatest Sporting Moments of All Time.*

20 Greatest Sporting Moments of All Time

This book will allow you to relive the 20 greatest sporting moments in history as if you were watching them all over again.

Paragon Publishing

been derived from various sources. Please consult a licensed professional before attempting any techniques outlined in this book.

By reading this document, the reader agrees that under no circumstances is the author responsible for any losses, direct or indirect, that are incurred because of the use of the information contained within this document, including, but not limited to, errors, omissions, or inaccuracies.

Table of Contents

Introduction 8

Chapter 1: Tiger Woods Winning the Masters in 2019 10

Chapter 2: Manchester City Winning the 2011–2012 English Premier League 13

Chapter 3: Germany Thrashing Brazil 7-1 in 2014 FIFA World Cup Semi-Final in Brazil 17

Chapter 4: Buster Douglas Knocking Out Mike Tyson 20

Chapter 5: Super Bowl LI in 2017 23

Chapter 6: South Africa Winning the Rugby World Cup in 1995 26

Chapter 7: Arsenal's Unbeaten English Premier League Win in 2003–2004 33

Chapter 8: The Rumble in the Jungle 37

Chapter 9: Leicester City's English Premier League Winning Campaign, 2015–2016 40

Chapter 10: The Red Sox Winning the World Series in 2004 43

Chapter 11: Jesse Owens Taking Berlin by Storm at the 1936 Olympics 46

Chapter 12: Liverpool Clinching the Champions League in 2005 50

Chapter 13: Roger Bannister Breaking the Four-Minute Mile in 1954 53

Chapter 14: Derek Redmond Finishing with His Father's Help, 1992 .... **56**

Chapter 15: Michael Jordan Taking "The Shot" in 1989 .. **59**

Chapter 16: Federer vs. Nadal in the 2008 Wimbledon Final **62**

Chapter 17: Usain Bolt at the 2008 Beijing Olympic Games.

Chapter 18: Michael Phelps Breaking Gold Medal Record in 2008 .... **66**

Chapter 19: Simone Biles Becoming the Most Decorated Gymnast of All-Time **70**

Chapter 20: Emma Raducanu Winning the US Open **73**

Conclusion **76**

References **78**

Introduction

If magic does exist, then it definitely exists in sports. Sports have produced magic time and time again. Whether it be football (soccer), American football, baseball, running, swimming, tennis, gymnastics, boxing, basketball, or golf is irrelevant, as you are bound to see moments of magic no matter the sport.

Although many magical moments have left sports fans bewildered and asking, "did that just happen?", there are simply moments of sports history that rank higher on the hierarchy of the greatest moments in sporting history. Twenty of these moments stand out from the rest, and they have been hand-picked and highlighted here. These moments were selected not only due to the magic that they produced but also the legacy, significance, and influence they left in the history of sports.

Moments such as Michael Phelps raking in gold medals at the 2008 Beijing Olympics, the New England Patriots pulling off possibly the greatest comeback in history, Simone Biles smashing the world gymnastics medal record at just 22, and Germany destroying Brazil 7-1 in the 2014 FIFA World Cup semi-final will all be remembered forever due to the sheer magic of these moments. Other incredible performances that will never be forgotten due to the brilliance that was on display include when Liverpool won the 2005 UEFA Champions League in dramatic fashion against a star-studded AC Milan, Arsenal's "invincible" season in 2004, Manchester City pulling off the most nail-biting English First Division League Championship in 2012, Michael Jordan's "The Shot" versus the Cavaliers, the Federer versus Nadal 2008 Wimbledon final, and Usain Bolt's masterclass at the 2008 Beijing Olympics.

However, while these moments have just been mentioned due to their sheer brilliance, some moments have been included for their absolute magic as well as representing something even bigger than the moment itself. These moments include South Africa's Springboks helping unify a once racially oppressed and segregated nation through rugby, Leicester City defying 5000/1 odds to win the English Premier League, Tiger Woods' return to golf's elite, the Boston Red Sox breaking an 86-year World Series curse, a supposedly "washed-up" Mohammed Ali knocking out the seemingly unbeatable George Foreman for the heavyweight title, and Emma Raducanu's rise from being an unknown to becoming the US Open Champion.

Wherever you look in this book, you will find moments of pure amazement and sometimes disbelief that these events happened. These are moments that anyone can enjoy, admire, and find inspiration from regardless of whether they are a fan of sports or not.

Chapter 1: Tiger Woods Winning the Masters in 2019

The 2019 Masters at the Augusta National Golf Course produced scenes of one of the most emotional finishes in the tournament's history when Tiger Woods won his fifth green jacket at 43 years old. That was the year when golf's prodigal son reclaimed his seat at the throne in golfing royalty. It was the tournament where the world got to see the Tiger Woods of old for the first time in nearly 15 years since he last won The Masters and 11 years since he won a major.

It is no secret he is one of the greatest golfers of all time, if not the greatest. Woods bossed the golfing world in the 1990s and 2000s. He was untouchable, a prodigy like no other, and a superstar who was not only an iconic name in golf but an iconic name in sports worldwide. Thus, when Woods' back injuries and personal life began to impede his abilities in the late 2000s, it was hard to watch as it was one of the saddest declines in sporting history.

Woods went from being a golfing superstar to slowly becoming almost irrelevant in the golfing world between the late 2000s and virtually all the 2010s. A main reason for this was his back injuries. By the time the 2019 Masters came around, he had already had four back surgeries. Woods was also often involved in many scandals in the media, and his personal life. Many believed Tiger's career was over and that he would never be able to perform anywhere near to the levels that he so often did in the 1990s and early 2000s. However, Tiger proved them wrong in the 2019 Masters with a breathtaking display and signaling his return to being one of golf's finest players once again.

The Tiger Woods of the past was not used to rallying to win major championships as it simply wasn't in his DNA before the 2019 Masters. In all of Tiger's previous major wins, he was either leading or level after 54 holes. However, this time he was battling it out with an Italian golfer, Francesco Molinari, who got the better of Woods just one year earlier at the British Open (Westin, 2019).

Molinari was in the lead after the first 11 holes, but his grip was loosened when he scuffed his shot on the 12th hole as it was short and rolled back into Rae's Creek. This led to the Italian having to settle for a double bogey, which meant he would now be tied with Woods at 11 under par. At the 15th hole, Molinari and Woods were tied at -12; however, Molinari hit his ball into the water, and Woods made a birdie, putting him at the top position (Patterson, 2019).

Woods was now in front and had the momentum. He doubled his advantage on the 16th hole. At the 17th hole, Woods's tee shot came within inches of going in, stopping just three feet from the hole for an easy tap-in. Finally, there was just the 18th hole left to stop Woods from returning to glory.

All he needed was a bogey to clinch his fifth green jacket. Woods expertly made bogey and won his first major in 11 years after trailing for 54 holes. The scenes were glorious as the world once again witnessed the brilliance of Tiger Woods.

Chapter 2: Manchester City Winning the 2011–2012 English Premier League

The English Premier League's 2011–2012 season will go down in history as the most iconic season in English league football history, due to the nature of how it finished. It was a nail-biter from when the season kicked off in August 2011 right through to its conclusion in May 2012. It was the season of the Manchester rivalry between the sky blue of Manchester City and the blood red of Manchester United. Everybody knew that the title of English Premier league holders for the 2011–2012 season would be awarded to Manchester, but which Manchester club would it be? The final day of the season fell on May 13, 2012, and both Manchester clubs would play their respective fixtures at the same time on a Sunday at 4:00 p.m. Manchester City was at home versus QPR, and Manchester United was away versus Sunderland.

It was Manchester City's title to lose as, although both clubs were sitting on 86 points come the final day of the season, Manchester City had a superior goal difference of +63 as opposed to Manchester United's +55. All Manchester City had to do was win their final game, and then, even if Manchester United won their game against Sunderland, Manchester City's goal difference would be enough to ensure they got their hands on the 2011–2012 English Premier League trophy for the first time in 44 years.

The whistles blew for kick-offs and both Manchester clubs began their final fixtures of their games. Manchester City started off quite conservatively and struggled to get a hold of the fixture from the get-go. They controlled the possession but were lacking the ruthless finishing product that they had showcased often throughout the season.

Twenty minutes passed for both Manchester fixtures, and Manchester United scored first against their Sunderland opponents on a Wayne Rooney goal that ensured Manchester United would not only go ahead of the match against Sunderland but also ensure that they would now be two points clear of their Manchester rivals at the top spot of the league table (McNulty, 2012).

However, Manchester City soon scored a goal of their own through their Argentina full-back Pablo Zabaleta in the 39th minute to put Manchester City up 1-0 against QPR and regain the top spot of the league table, leading Manchester United on goal difference. The situation for Manchester City took a turn for the worse early in the second half when QPR's talisman Djibril Cisse scored an equalizer in the 48th minute. The score was now 1-1, and Manchester United had once again regained the top spot two points clear of Manchester City.

Another turn of events unfolded in the Manchester City match when QPR's Joey Barton received a red card for a horrible challenge on Carlos Tevez and then kicked Sergio Aguero after being given his marching orders to leave the field. QPR was now down to 10 men, and this was Manchester City's opportunity to take advantage of a weakened QPR side—or not. QPR miraculously managed to go ahead of Manchester City with a second goal even with 10 men, thanks to a strike from Jamie Mackie. Now, Manchester United was three points clear of Manchester City on the league standings with just 24 minutes of regulation time remaining.

Manchester City failed to score, despite their best efforts for the rest of regulation time, and so the game moved into injury time. Within minutes of starting injury time, a miracle occurred. Edin Dzeko equalized for Manchester City in the 92nd minute, and now Manchester City was just two points away from clinching the league title. Three minutes of injury time remained, and the spirits of the blue-clad fans of Manchester skyrocketed.

It was a long shot, but the Manchester City players and fans dared to dream and, believe it or not, their dreams were materialized in the 95th minute when Aguero banged in the winning goal for Manchester City, thus clinching the 3-2 win and firmly grasping the 2011–2012 English Premier League title. The second Aguero's strike found the back of the net, the cries of "Agueeeeeeeeeeero" could be heard through millions of television sets around the world.

The Etihad was an explosion of sky blue as Aguero took his shirt off and swung it above his head as he and thousands upon thousands of Manchester City fans celebrated the league title after 44 years of frustration that had finally come to an end. It was a moment of magic that only sports can provide (McNulty, 2012).

Chapter 3: Germany Thrashing Brazil 7-1 in 2014 FIFA World Cup Semi-Final in Brazil

Bizarre, absolutely bizarre. There simply isn't another adjective that can truly capture the essence of this iconic moment in football and FIFA World Cup history. Germany demolished Brazil in the 2014 FIFA World Cup semi-final on July 8, 2014, in Belo Horizonte. Now, to truly grasp why this result is so iconic, one needs to understand that Brazil simply does not lose 7-1 to any team, not even to the best teams in the world; it is unheard of. What is even more unheard of is for Brazil to lose 7-1 at home. To add to why this result seems even stranger than fiction is that this all occurred in a semi-final of a FIFA World Cup that Brazil was hosting. A 7-1 defeat is the biggest defeat in a semi-final in FIFA world cup history, and what is even more astounding is that the victim of this goal-scoring assault from Germany was Brazil, who was not only the host of the tournament but also the most successful nation in FIFA world cup history.

This was no ordinary Brazil side either. Brazil was one of the favorites, if not the favorite, to bring the World Cup home for the sixth time to add to their unparalleled success as a nation in the tournament's history. This was a star-studded Brazilian side with players in their prime years such as Marcelo, Dani Alves, Oscar, Willian, Hulk, Maicon, Fernandinho, Dante, Julio Cesar, David Luiz, and Ramires. These were household names that played week in and week out for the best clubs in world football; however, it is fair to say that Brazil was without its star Neymar for this fixture, which was a huge blow to the Brazilians, considering that Neymar was arguably one of the top five best players in the world at that time. Nevertheless, Neymar's absence does not justify the 7-1 drubbing by the Germans.

While this was a star-studded Brazilian side, they were also up against the would-be champions of the 2014 FIFA World Cup, Germany, and its lineup was filled with superstars and household names that represented the best clubs in the world week in and week out. The Germans had players at the peak of their footballing abilities such as Ozil, Muller, Lahm, Kroos, Neuer, Schweinsteiger, Kroos, Boateng, and Hummels. On paper, it looked like a match that would be very difficult to choose from and that it would be a hard-fought cagey affair that would be decided by one goal, maybe two at most. This, however, was far from the case.

As the Mexican referee, Marco Rodriguez, blew the first whistle for kickoff, Germany hit the ground running and took control of the fixture. It was clear to see which side was hungrier for the win and which side came out the tunnel more ruthless than the other side.

Within 11 minutes, Thomas Muller drew first blood for Germany and the fans could sense the Germans were hungry for more. In the 23rd minute, the floodgates opened when Germany's talisman Klose scored the second goal of the match. What followed was an onslaught. Just one minute after Klose's goal, Toni Kroos scored Germany's third in the 24th minute, and just two minutes later in the 26th minute, Kroos doubled his tally and propelled the Germans to a 4-0 lead. Three minutes later in the 29th minute, Sami Khedira scored Germany's fifth goal. Thus, within just seven minutes, Germany had put four goals in the back of the Brazilian net.

Germany went into halftime 5-0 up, and the Germans knew now that they had booked their ticket to the World Cup final, while the Brazilians entered the changing rooms at halftime gutted and their spirits crushed. Marco Rodriguez blew the whistle for the second half, and Germany picked up where they left off by scoring two more goals in the 69th and 79th minutes courtesy of their talented forward substitute Andre Schurrle. Finally, in the 90th minute, Oscar scored a consolation goal to end the match at 7-1. Oscar's goal was not enough to save the Brazilians from utter embarrassment or prevent the hosts from ending their 2014 FIFA World Cup journey.

Chapter 4: Buster Douglas Knocking Out Mike Tyson

Buster Douglas, the underdog boxer who knocked out boxing's golden boy Mike Tyson is truly an inspiring tale. Douglas was the heavy underdog in this bout and was virtually given no chance of beating the heavyweight champion of the world at the time, Mike Tyson. Not only did Douglas have all odds against him with the bookies placing the odds of Douglas beating Tyson at 42-1, but just 23 days before the fight, Douglas's mother died suddenly, leaving the title challenger shocked and in grief. Lula Douglas died shockingly from a stroke, and Buster had to bury his beloved mother just days before he had to catch a flight to Japan to participate in the most important night of his life for his title shot with Iron Mike (Jones, 2018).

Due to the already terrible odds of Buster winning the fight being paired with the shocking loss of his mother, the boxing world didn't even think Buster would last 30 seconds in the ring. His father, dealing with the grief of losing his wife, urged his son to fight and give it all he had. He told Buster, "Let your hand go and see what happens" and that's exactly what Buster did, and in hindsight, that piece of advice won him the heavyweight title in the fight of his life.

Meanwhile, Tyson and his corner team, knowing that he was the obvious favorite to win the fight, was arrogant, so arrogant that they didn't even bring an ice pack to reduce swelling during the breaks between rounds (Jones, 2018). Do not be mistaken, Douglas was a talented boxer, but too often he would fall short in big fights, which are the kind of fights that define a boxer's career. However, that would all change on February 11, 1990.

As soon as the bell rang for the first round, Douglas fought the fight of his life with no fear and took the fight straight to Tyson. Douglas threw perfect combinations and showed great defensive qualities and was battering the heavyweight champion of the world with strong tactful punches. Douglas was in control and Tyson failed to pull off any consistent attacks.

By the fourth round, Tyson had bad swelling around his eyes. Douglas continued to win round after round, as he was on the offensive and consistently applying pressure on Tyson with beautiful combination punches. However, Tyson was not ready to give in just yet and in the eight-round managed to counter with an extremely powerful right uppercut that brought Douglas to the canvas (Casiano, 2020). Douglas got up and beat the 10 count and became even more ruthless than before.

Douglas won the 9th round by continuing to beat up Tyson and in the 10th round knocked out Tyson with a right uppercut followed by a barrage of punches. Tyson hit the canvas and could not get up before the count of

10. A new heavyweight champion was crowned, and when Douglas was asked how he won a fight seemingly impossible to win, he responded "because of my mother, God bless her heart" (Jones, 2018).

Chapter 5: Super Bowl LI in 2017

Super Bowl LI in 2017 was one of the greatest comeback stories ever in the National Football League (NFL). It was a story of grit and determination. A story of character and finding the spark needed to win even when the chips were down when the New England Patriots played the Atlanta Falcons.

The Super Bowl kicked off, and the game remained scoreless in the first quarter of play after a defensive showcase from both New England and Atlanta with both franchises punting twice. Atlanta's Deion Jones stripped the ball from the Patriots' running back LeGarrette Blount, causing a fumble that was snatched up by Atlanta's Robert Alford. The Falcons now had the ball, and on the next two plays, quarterback Matt Ryan threw passes to gain 19 and 23 yards (New England Patriots, 2017). In the next three plays, the Falcons managed to cover the remaining 29 yards and score the first touchdown of the game and go 7-0 ahead. Soon, the Falcons moved the ball another 62 yards in just five plays and scored another touchdown for a 14-0 lead over New England.

Things were about to go from bad to worse for the Patriots as quarterback Tom Brady threw a wayward pass that was intercepted for an 82-yard return by the Falcons' Alford for the third touchdown. The score was 21-0 for Atlanta, and it looked like that would be the score going into half-time. The Patriots' Stephen

Gostkowski made the score 21-3 just two minutes before half-time.

In the third quarter following a New England punt, Atlanta began to drive the ball from their 15-yard line. Ryan successfully threw two long passes for 52 yards in total, bringing the ball to the Patriots' 28-yard line (Wikipedia, 2021e). Just six plays later, the Falcons scored their fourth touchdown, going 28-3 ahead thanks to Tevin Coleman.

With only 8:31 left in the third quarter, the whole world thought that Super Bowl LI had been decided. The game was seemingly over, but then a miracle happened. Tom Brady, being Tom Brady, found the answer for the Patriots as he had done countless times before. Brady and the Patriots covered 75 yards in the next 13 plays, leading to a game-changing touchdown. However, Gostkowski missed gaining the extra point when his kick hit the goal post.

In the fourth quarter, the Patriots had a field-goal opportunity with only 10 minutes remaining in the game. Gostkowski stepped up and his 33-yard field goal was good. The score was 28-12 and what once seemed impossible by the middle of the third quarter suddenly seemed possible, unlikely but possible. It went from bad to worse for Atlanta as they fumbled and the Patriots scored their second touchdown and made the two-point conversion to put the score at 28-20 (Wikipedia, 2021e).

With a minute to go in the game, Atlanta was closing in

on being crowned Super Bowl Champions, but with just 58 seconds on the clock, the Patriots scored a one-yard touchdown and completed a two-point conversion. The score was 28-28, the Patriots pulled off the impossible, and the game would be settled in overtime. After a fiercely competitive period of play in overtime from both teams, the Patriots scored another one-yard touchdown and won the game 34-28 after trailing by 25 points and being behind virtually the entire game. The Patriots stole the Super Bowl away from the Falcons in one of the most iconic games in NFL history.

Chapter 6: South Africa Winning the Rugby World Cup in 1995

The 1995 Rugby World Cup is a story that not even the greatest writers in Hollywood could muster up. It was pure magic, with so many layers behind the miraculous win that ensured the Springboks' (South African rugby team) first Rugby World Cup. To truly understand how magical and inspiring this achievement was for the Springboks, one needs to understand the background behind this awe-inspiring win.

South Africa just transitioned into a democratic country after the abolishment of several decades of racial oppression, segregation, and discrimination of non-white, particularly black, South Africans, during what was known as the Apartheid. The Apartheid was a system that existed to ensure white South Africans reigned supreme. Apartheid lasted from 1948 until 1994, although many believe that the Apartheid started several years before 1948. Thankfully due to the efforts of global support, countless freedom fighters, and the influence of Nelson Mandela, the Apartheid regime was abolished, and democracy was installed. Even though South Africa was now a democratic country, the new president, Nelson Mandela, faced many challenges such as extreme tension and unresolved issues that needed to be attended to. Racial tension was rife, the country was on the brink of a civil war, uncertainty was in the air, and the vision of Mandela's "Rainbow Nation" was met with skepticism, to say the least.

Mandela saw an opportunity in the 1995 Rugby World Cup to rectify all the issues that lay in his and South Africa's way. That opportunity came in the form of the Springboks. Mandela knew sports had the power to unite a nation, even a nation of enemies, and that's just what he did.

South Africa was the host of the 1995 World Cup. The Springboks had been isolated from playing rugby from the 1970s until 1992, thus the green and gold were seriously out of practice. This was the first Rugby World Cup the Springboks were eligible to compete in, and they were considered a 'weak' team compared to the other nations. Thus, the odds were not in their favor. As the World Cup grew closer to its inauguration, a visual change could be seen in South Africa and Mandela's vision to unify the country through sports began to unfold beautifully.

The tournament commenced on May 25, 1995, and contrary to the world's doubts, South Africa won every match leading to the final. The Springboks finished at the top of their group by beating one of the tournament favorites, Australia, 27-18 in Cape Town. The Boks went on to beat Western Samoa in the quarter-finals and narrowly beat France in an iconic match 19-15 in heavy rainfall in Durban. Finally, the Springboks had reached the final and what seemed impossible had become a reality, since not only did the Boks reach the final, but their road to the final sparked unification of a country that had been segregated for decades.

South Africa played New Zealand in the final at Ellis Park, Johannesburg. New Zealand was the obvious favorite, but South Africa had proven so many times already that they were not to be underestimated. In the first half, no tries were scored, however, that did not take away from the tense atmosphere of the game. The Springboks were playing defensively throughout the first half as New Zealand was on the offensive as the All Blacks (New Zealand's Rugby team) usually are. Still, every effort by the All Blacks was denied. After several penalties were awarded to both sides, the half-time ended with South Africa leading 9-6. All points for South Africa were scored by the boot of Joel Stransky and the points for New Zealand were scored by Andrew Mehrtens (Cleary & Donegan, 1995).

The second half was much of the same as the All Blacks were on the offensive and the Springboks were on the defensive. In the 55th minute, Mehrtens equalized for New Zealand and the score read 9-9. Mehrtens almost clinched the final for the All Blacks with a drop goal but narrowly missed. Thus, the final would go into extra-time.

In the first half of extra-time, both teams were awarded penalties and both Stransky and Mehretens slotted them home, leveling the score at 12-12 at the end of the first half of extra time.

In the second half of extra-time, a miracle happened,

as with just seven minutes left of play, Joel Stransky scored a drop goal from 30meters out to put the Springboks 15-12 ahead and this would prove to be enough to ensure South Africa won their first-ever Rugby World Cup and unified Mandela's Rainbow Nation as a democratic and harmonious nation.

When an interviewer asked the Springboks' captain Francois Pienaar what it felt like to win in front of 65,000 people, Pienaar ironically replied, "We didn't have 65,000, we had 43 million" (Rothman, 2015).

Chapter 7: Arsenal's Unbeaten English Premier League Win in 2003–2004

The 2003–2004 English Premier League season was Arsenal's finest season in their illustrious history, and perhaps the finest season by any English club in football history. Arsenal's 2003–2004 season was the pinnacle of success and is considered the perfect season. This season is so iconic that it was awarded the nickname the "Invincible season," and the squad that achieved this outrageous feat is known simply as the 'Invincibles.'

The only other club that achieved an unbeaten status throughout an entire season is Preston North End in the 1888–1889 English league season. However, back then, a season was only 27 games, and the season Arsenal achieved their unbeaten status was in a 38-game season (Hughes, 2004).

Thus, no English club in the 100 years or to this day has gone undefeated for an entire season in the English domestic top-flight league. The achievement is truly astonishing and so unique that when Arsenal won the 2003–2004 English Premier League, they were awarded a gold trophy. This is the only gold English league trophy that has ever been awarded, and it sits comfortably in the highly impressive trophy room in the Emirates, the home of London's most successful football club.

What makes this season so incredible is not only that this Arsenal side went an entire season undefeated, but the sheer determination, character, and consistency of this star-studded squad. Even if the Gunners were not playing particularly well in a particular fixture, they would somehow manage to ensure to escape defeat and that's what the best clubs in the world do—they make sure that they never walk away empty-handed, as even if it is just a draw, they will still walk away with at least one point. Arsenal did this time and time again in the 2003–2004 season. They always found an answer and they always delivered. Whether it was a stellar performance by Arsenal's world-class forwards, bossing the game in midfield, or producing a performance of impenetrable defense, it did not matter. Arsenal found the answer and they had concocted a winning formula that no club could crack.

The Invincibles were filled to the brim with unbelievable talent. Names such as Henry, Bergkamp, Kolo Toure, Pires, Viera, Ashley Cole, Campbell and more, were feared by every club and supporter across England and Europe. They had no weaknesses, no position that could be targeted as their Achilles heel. They were one of the most balanced squads in football history. They had players that could walk into any club in world football, and on top of that, they had one of the greatest managers the football world has ever seen: Arsene Wegner. They truly were an unstoppable force.

They ended the season with an astonishing 26 wins, 12 draws, and 0 defeats in a 38-match season. Thus, they ended the season as undefeated champions with 90 points, leading second place by 11 points.

Chapter 8: The Rumble in the Jungle

Youth versus experience. Power versus speed. That is exactly what "The Rumble in the Jungle" was. On October 30, 1974, two of boxing's all-time greats, George Foreman and Mohammed Ali battled it out in Zaire (now known as the Democratic Republic of Congo). The fight between these two iconic legends was billed as one of the greatest fights in boxing history and, truth be told, it was.

At the time, the heavyweight boxing champion, George Foreman, was in the prime of his life at 25 years old. He was a youthful, powerful, knockout machine that would see his opponents hit the canvas nine times out of 10. Foreman was seen as invincible. In fact, before The Rumble in the Jungle, Forman was undefeated with 40 wins of which 37 were knockouts. Foreman demolished boxers who had given Ali trouble in the past, most notably Foreman knocked out Smokin' Joe Frazier in the second round in 1973 to win the WBC and WBA World Heavyweight titles (Classic Boxing Matches, 2016).

On the other hand, Ali, as legendary and skillful as he was, was aging and already 32. He was not as powerful as Foreman nor was he at the same physical peak of his ability as Foreman, but he was fast, full of stamina (despite his age), and he had more experience in the ring than his opponent Foreman. The boxing world had written off Ali for this fight. He was the heavy underdog, considered to be past his best, too old, and simply not as powerful as his Hercules-like opponent Foreman. It is hard to believe that Ali, the greatest heavyweight boxer of all time, was given almost no chance of winning this fight according to bookies and the boxing world.

Ali was stripped of his heavyweight title in 1967 for political reasons as he refused to take any part in the Vietnam War. Ali went into exile from boxing until the early 1970s, and when he returned to regain the title from Joe Frazier, he lost in a shock defeat by a unanimous decision by the judges after 15 rounds in 1971 (Classic Boxing Matches, 2016).

Hence, when The Rumble in the Jungle's bell rang to signal the first round, Ali was hungry to regain the heavyweight title and prove all his doubters wrong. *The Rumble in the Jungle* was not a fight filled with extraordinary boxing skill, however. It was a fight that showed a bold yet genius strategy from Ali, and that was to tire out the bigger, stronger, and more sluggish Foreman who was used to knocking out his opponents in the first couple rounds. Thus, Ali knew that if he could survive the first four rounds of Foreman's onslaught, then the fight would be Ali's to win.

Naturally, the fight began with Foreman bringing the fight to Ali and essentially pummeling the living hell out of the former champion. However, somehow Ali managed to absorb Foreman's brutal punches like a sponge and come out virtually unscathed. It was unbelievable. Any other boxer would have hit the canvas after Foreman's onslaught of punches, yet Ali encouraged Foreman to keep on throwing punches to tire himself out. This was all part of Ali's incredible strategy that worked as the rounds went on. Foreman became more and more sluggish and was paying the price of his own exhaustion, while Ali, although being on the wrong end of Foreman's assault in the first four rounds or so, was still full of energy and roaring to go. Foreman was exhausted, and now Ali brought the fight to him, and as the rounds passed, Ali took charge of the fight, and suddenly the extreme underdog had transitioned into the predator, not the prey.

As the fight reached the eighth round, Foreman's punching and defense were almost non-existent due to sheer exhaustion. Ali knew this was the round he would end the fight and reclaim the heavyweight title. Foreman tried to pin Ali to the ropes to slow the fight down, but then Ali pounced and delivered the greatest combination of knockout punches of all time. The five-punch combination from Ali started after a Foreman jab. Ali threw two hard left hooks, then another left hook that brought Foreman's face into position for the perfectly delivered right hook, followed by a strong jab to Foreman's face (Crean, 2021).

Ali won the fight against all the odds and became just the second man in history at the time to regain the heavyweight title. This fight showed just how well Ali could withstand multiple hard punches and his tactical genius as one of the smartest boxers of all time.

Chapter 9: Leicester City's English Premier League Winning Campaign, 2015–2016

To anyone who believes fairytales do not exist, think again, because in May 2016 one of the greatest fairytales of all time took place: Leicester City won the 2015–2016 English Premier League (EPL) against 5000/1 odds (Vasilogambros, 2016).

It is unthinkable that a club like Leicester City overcame these ridiculous odds in one of, if not the most difficult and competitive leagues of all time. Yet somehow the Foxes pulled off the greatest fairytale in football history. Just one season before their miraculous title-winning season, Leicester narrowly escaped relegation from English top-flight football. They survived the drop by only five points and went on to win the most prestigious domestic league title in world football 12 months later. Not even the most optimistic and die-hard Leicester City fans could have envisioned their beloved club qualifying for Champions League football, perhaps not even Europa League football. But never in a million years would they think the same side that narrowly escaped the drop just 12 months earlier would be crowned the kings of English football.

This was a side that was competing with some of the wealthiest clubs in world football. Clubs like Manchester City, Manchester United, and Chelsea had seemingly bottomless pockets when it came to acquiring the world's finest footballing talent. Leicester, on the other hand, was on the opposite spectrum. They were one of the "poorest" clubs in the English Premier League at the start of the 2015 summer transfer window and were forced to acquire players from less prestigious leagues and clubs. Some players were not even playing in the topflight of their respective leagues. However, Leicester did manage to strike gold, even if they were shopping at the dollar store for players, as they managed to bring in N'golo Kante (arguably the best midfielder in the world today), Robert Huth, Okazaki, Fuchs, and Damarai Gray who all played integral parts for Leicester's title-winning campaign (Ronay, 2016).

However, they had some fantastic talent of their own besides these summer transfer acquisitions who miraculously transitioned from virtual unknowns to global superstars: Jamie Vardy, Riyad Mahrez, Danny Drinkwater, Wes Morgan, and Kasper Schmeichel (the son of Peter Schmeichel, who is arguably in the top five best goalkeepers of all time). Thus, Leicester's unknowns began racking up wins week after week, and the question on everyone's lips was "When will the bubble burst, as surely they cannot run on this type of form all season; eventually, they will plummet?" However, the Foxes never did, and they were ruthless throughout the entire 2015–2016 campaign right up until they lifted the English Premier League trophy in May 2016.

Leicester City ended the season with 23 wins, 12 draws, and just 3 losses! A simply outstanding record. Not only would Leicester finish in the top spot at the end of the 2015–2016 EPL season, but they would finish as comfortable champions with 81 points, which were 10 points ahead of second-place Arsenal, who finished with 71 points (Ronay, 2016).

It was a season that optimized the saying "dare to dream." This season is why so many people around the world love football and other sports, due to the magic that they bring and the essence that anybody or any team can win no matter the odds. The legacy of the 2015–2016 EPL season has inspired "so-called" smaller clubs in the EPL to up their game and competitiveness, and it has consistently been seen in seasons that have preceded Leicester City's title-winning campaign that the English Premier League lower-table clubs have upped their game. The legacy it left is that no game in the EPL can be considered an easy fixture.

Chapter 10: The Red Sox Winning the World Series in 2004

The 2004 World Series would finally see the Red Sox lift the "Curse of the Bambino," which was a nickname for the supposedly endless drought of 86 years since the Red Sox won the World Series (Kory, 2014). The last time the Red Sox won the World Series was in 1918, and the following season, the Red Sox sold arguably the greatest of all time (GOAT) of baseball players to their fierce rivals the New York Yankees. Many believed that the selling of Babe Ruth was the start of the "Curse of the Bambino" for the Red Sox.

The 2004 World Series signaled the 100th edition of the competition and would be played by the St. Louis Cardinals against the underdogs the Boston Red Sox in a seven-game series for the World Series title. The Red Sox reached the World Series by winning the American League championship series by beating the New York Yankees. The Red Sox lost the first three games to the Yankees but came back to beat the Yankees in four straight games to win the series. In contrast, the Cardinals swept the Houston Astros in the National League championship series.

The seven-game World series was heavily analyzed and was an extremely difficult series to call. Many analysts had differing opinions, and there were no clear favorites as the predictions were almost split down the middle with some backing Boston and some backing St. Louis. However, what was interesting is how so many baseball pundits and journalists noted how unexpected both teams were in terms of reaching the World Series in the first place. It was said that these teams were not the strongest franchises in the United States at the time and that other teams on paper were quite a fair share stronger, yet both the Cardinals and the Red Sox would be battling it out for the World Series from October 23 to October 27, 2004. *Sports Illustrated's* John Donovan went as far as to say these franchises were "not supposed to be here" and praised both teams' resilience and spirit to reach the World Series so unexpectedly (Kory, 2014). Although the World Series was an extremely difficult one to call, the Red Sox would go into the World Series with just a little bit of an edge over the Cardinals as Boston was awarded home-field advantage due to winning the All-Star game. This meant that the Red Sox would have home advantage at Fenway Park for four out of seven games.

Although the Red Sox had home-field advantage, nobody expected them to be so dominant in the first three games of the World Series. The Red Sox went on to win the first three games of the series. They won the first game 11-9 at Fenway Park, the second game 6-2 at Fenway Park, and the third game 4-1 at Busch Stadium. Thus, the Red Sox were 3-0 up in the series. One game stood in their way to finally lift the "Curse of the Bambino," and Boston knew that just one more win would clinch the World Series and end their 86-year drought.

In the fourth game of the World Series at Busch Stadium, the Red Sox's Johnny Damon smashed a home run at the first at-bat of the game, giving the Red Sox an early 1-0 lead. The Red Sox soon added to their lead after doubles by David Oritz and Trot Nixon, which drove in two more runs, putting them 3-0 in the fourth game of thc series (Kory, 2014). This would prove pivotal as those runs would decide the fate of the World Series and see Boston finally being crowned World Series Champions for the first time since 1918. Despite the best efforts of the Cardinals, they could not break down the Red Sox's brilliant defense and the fourth game ended 3-0 to Boston. The Red Sox were now World Series Champions, and they did it in style by winning the World Series 4-0. The Red Sox had returned to baseball's finest franchises and a new era was born.

Chapter 11: Jesse Owens Taking Berlin by Storm at the 1936 Olympics

Jesse Owens is a true American hero; in fact, he is a true global hero. Owens is the personification of resilience, sheer will, optimism, and outrageous talent. He is a black icon and an inspiration to not only athletes but to minorities all over the world. Owens ran at a time when black Americans were discriminated against, prejudiced against, denied equal opportunities, and seen as second-rate citizens in the U.S. in the 1930s. Thus, it came as a huge surprise to America and the world when an extremely talented and youthful superstar black runner by the name of Jesse Owens came through the ranks of the running world in the U.S. and was seen as the USA's golden boy for the 1936 Berlin Olympics. This was simply unheard of.

Owens proved to the U.S. that racial discrimination and any form of racism had no place in the world, that we should be considered as human beings and not judged by the color of our skin. Owens broke down racial boundaries in America, maybe not completely, but in a way that gave African Americans hopes and dreams. He sparked a notion that one day the African American oppression in the U.S. would come to an end and minorities and white Americans could live together harmoniously.

Owens' talent qualified him for the 1936 Berlin Olympics, and he won America's heart with his superhuman speed and athletic abilities. The whole of the U.S. was rooting for Jesse Owens. They never saw him as a black runner. They saw him as a runner with impressive talent. By Owens achieving that feat alone to just be seen as another athlete and not a black athlete was worth more than any Olympic medal. However, his racial oppression and discrimination did not begin and end in the United States as he was about to travel to Berlin, which was arguably even more discriminatory towards black people under the leadership of the infamous Adolf Hitler.

Just as Jesse Owens won the hearts of Americans, he won the hearts of the world at the 1936 Berlin Olympics. He did it on one of the most unlikely stages in an Olympics hosted by Nazi Germany, which was extremely strict (to say the least) on what was considered acceptable and unacceptable. On top of that, Hitler was advocating how the Aryan race would sweep up all the medals at the 1936 Olympics due to the German dictator's perceived notion that Aryans were the supreme specimens of the living world. This didn't faze Jesse Owens, and he would go on to win four Olympic gold medals and break three Olympic records in Berlin in 1936, an achievement that is almost unthinkable to even attempt. Owens disputed the notion of the Aryan race's superiority by stealing the show in Berlin.

Jesse Owens tied the 100-meter record of 10.3 seconds to win his first gold. Next, Owens set his first Olympic record in the 200-meter race, finishing in 20.7 seconds to win his second gold. If that was not impressive enough, he set another record and snatched up his third gold medal in Berlin by jumping a record 26 feet and 5¼ inches in the long-jump event. Finally, Owen won his fourth gold medal and set a new record with his relay team with the American's finishing in 39.8 seconds in the 400-meter relay (Ohio State University, 2020).

What makes Jesse Owens' performance at the 1936 Berlin Olympics even more impressive is that being a track and field athlete in the 1930s was a lot tougher than it is today. That is not taking anything away from modern athletes, but in the 1936 Olympics there were no starting blocks, running shoes were far heavier due to the leather used, the running tracks were not turf tracks, and cinders made the tracks uneven (Ohio State University, 2020). The tracks were also messy and slippery when it rained and, believe it or not, when Owens won his medals for sprinting, it was raining intermittently (Ohio State University, 2020).

Owens showed the world it did not matter what color your skin is, it did not matter where you were born, and it did not matter who the athlete is, the only thing that mattered is that sports are for everybody no matter who they are. He inspired the world and paved the way for athletes and sports stars of color to have future equal sporting opportunities.

Chapter 12: Liverpool Clinching the Champions League in 2005

If you are skeptical of miracles, then events that unfolded in Istanbul on May 25, 2005, may just change your perspective on the matter. That night is a night that will live in Liverpool Football Club and football folklore for eternity. It was a magical night, and if you are a Liverpool fan or a football fan in general, then the 2005 Champions League final between Liverpool and AC Milan will be a game you would have heard of and a match that you will continue to hear of for years and years to come.

After a grueling road to the Champions League final for both AC Milan and Liverpool, the two European giants were finally set to battle it out for European club football's grandest prize. It was no easy road to the final either. Liverpool had to overcome some of the strongest sides in world football, beating Bayern Leverkusen, Juventus, and Chelsea in the proceeding knockout rounds to stamp their ticket to partake in the final. AC Milan didn't have a smoother journey to the final, having to beat Manchester United, Inter Milan, and an extremely talented PSV side. However, both European giants overcame these roadblocks and were set to face off in the most exhilarating and nail-biting Champions League final of all time.

Although Liverpool boasted a strong side with some fantastic players like Gerrard, Xavi Alonso, Carragher, Hyypia, Baros, and Riise, they were simply outmatched by AC Milan's squad packed to the brim with some of football's best global superstars. AC Milan's line-up included legendary players like Kaka, Pirlo, Crespo, Gattuso, Seedorf, Maldini, Nesta, Staam, Cafu, Shevchenko, and Dida. This was one of the best AC Milan squads in history and had a habit of ripping apart even the best clubs in world football. Thus, before kickoff, it was clear that AC Milan was the favorite.

The whistle blew for kick-off, and Liverpool's worst nightmare became a reality. Within 50 seconds, AC Milan pulled ahead of Liverpool with a beautiful 12-yard volley struck by Maldini who made perfect contact from a Pirlo free-kick delivery as the ball flew through a sea of players into the back of the net (Glendenning, 2005). Almost one minute played and 1-0 to AC Milan against the less favoured Liverpool. Soon, things went from bad to worse for Liverpool. Crespo would go on to score two more goals for AC Milan in the 39th and 44th minutes, ensuring a 3-0 lead for the Italian side at half-time.

At halftime, the footballing world had already assumed that AC Milan had won the 2005 Champions League in just 45 minutes! However, Liverpool manager Rafa Benitez and his highly resilient squad had other ideas and refused to go down without a fight. As the whistle blew for the second half, the most incredible comeback in Champions League and football history was about to unfold.

Perhaps AC Milan took their foot off the gas as they thought the match had already been won, but Steven Gerrard, Liverpool's savior on so many occasions, pounced on the AC Milan players' laissez-faire attitude in the second half, clawing Liverpool back into the game with a goal of their own in the 54th minute with a game-changing header from six yards. The Liverpool captain, who had inspired his teammates on so many occasions had done it again and the skipper's goal inspired a miraculous comeback from the rest of Liverpool's players. Within minutes, Liverpool had drawn level with AC Milan with the score reading 3-3. First Vladimir Smicer scored a stunner from long range in the 56th minute, which was followed by an Alonso penalty that was initially saved by Dida, but the Spaniard managed to tap it in on the rebound (Glendenning, 2005). Liverpool had just pulled off the greatest comeback in European club football history in the space of eight minutes.

The next goal would decide the 2005 Champions League winner, and with all the momentum leaning towards Liverpool suddenly the heavy underdogs were now the favorites to win the final in Istanbul. However, despite the attacking efforts from both European clubs, neither club could find the clinical ruthlessness to penetrate the opposition defense for the rest of normal time and extra time. Thus, the whistle blew at 3-3 after 120 minutes, and it would be up to the fate of the dreaded penalty shootout to decide who would become the Kings of Europe in 2005. Liverpool would go on to win the penalty shootout 3-2 as AC Milan forgot their shooting boots at home missing three out of five penalties. Liverpool had won their fifth European trophy in their history by defying all the odds by bewildering AC Milan with one of the most outrageous comebacks in sporting history.

Chapter 13: Roger Bannister Breaking the Four-Minute Mile in 1954

Sir Roger Bannister did the seemingly impossible in 1954 and redefined what the human body could do when pushed to its limit. Bannister was the first person to run a mile in under four minutes. It was believed that the human body could not physically move that fast for such a distance. Scientists and running enthusiasts believed that the body would literally collapse under pressure, yet Bannister dared to dream and was determined to prove everybody wrong through achieving the so-called impossible.

Bannister was called crazy for even attempting such a feat, and what is even more extraordinary is that he would train unconventionally, often training for short periods compared to his competitors' rigorous training schedules. Bannister would only train for 30 minutes a day with intense speed workouts. He was only seconds off the four-minute mark in training, which gave him the confidence that if he pushed himself a little more, he could make history.

Before Douglas beat the one-mile world record, the record was set at a time of 4:01 minutes, not too far off from under four minutes, but if you're a runner, you will know just how long one second can be. However, even if it was a "literally" impossible record to break at the time, Bannister was determined to run a mile under four minutes.

On May 6, 1954, Banister would make history. While experts were adamant that running a mile under four minutes was impossible, they said theoretically it could only be broken on a day with no wind, temperature set at 20 degrees Celsius on a hard, dry, clay track in front of a crowd of 10,000 spectators (Runyon, 2014). These were the ideal conditions. However, May 6, 1954 had none of these ideal conditions.

Instead, the day Bannister broke the record for the fastest time in a mile, it was cold, and windy, the track was wet, and there were only about 3,000 spectators. Despite these supposedly unfavorable conditions, Bannister decided to run. There were six runners in this iconic race and, as soon as the race started, Bannister and his rival Basher took an early lead. Brasher would go on to lead for the first half of the race, while Banister was in second place with the third-place Chataway right on his tail. Soon enough, Chataway overtook Bannister who now found himself in third place. It was now down to the final lap and Bannister began the lap very slightly above three minutes, meaning he had to finish his final lap in less than 59 seconds. It seemed impossible, but Bannister miraculously flew past Chataway and Brasher on the last straight and, at that moment, he knew he made history. Bannister broke the record by finishing the mile in 3:59.4 seconds; he celebrated as the world stood still in awe.

Chapter 14: Derek Redmond Finishing with His Father's Help, 1992

The story of Derek Redmond at the 1992 Olympics in Barcelona is one of the most heart-warming moments in Olympic and sports history. It was a moment that truly showed how beautiful sports can be and how the bond between a father and son inspired the world. A story of will and determination. The story is that you must always finish what you started and that it is okay to get help along the way. It is a story that will live on for eternity in the minds and hearts of sports fans.

Redmond was an extremely talented runner and one of the world's greatest 400m specialists at the time. He broke the British record for the men's 400m finishing with a staggering time of 44.82 seconds in 1985. However, this record was broken two years later in 1987. This was a huge achievement and signaled that Redmond was a rising star the world should keep an eye on. The British runner would then go on to become one of the members of the British relay team in 1986, which won the gold medal in the 4 x 400m relay gold medal championship (Weinberg, 2004).

In 1991, Redmond was once again part of the 4 x 400m iconic British relay team that astoundingly beat the much more favored USA relay team to claim the gold at the 1991 World Championships. This was a fantastic performance by Redmond and his team as they posted the second-fastest 4 x 400m relay time in history (Weinberg, 2004).

However, despite all that Redmond had achieved throughout his career, he struggled with injuries. His progression as one of the world's greatest runners was too often interrupted by nagging injuries. He was forced to pull out of the 1988 Olympics in Seoul after he had injured his Achilles tendon within the first 90 seconds of his first race of the Olympics. This crushed Redmond, as it would any Olympian, as he was favored to win the gold for Britain if it were not for his unfortunate injury.

Although Redmond had to pull out of the 1988 Olympics, he had his eyes set on competing in the 1992 Olympics and coming back with a bang. Redmond trained hard for the Olympics in Barcelona, but injuries would not be kind to the talented British runner as once the 1992 Olympics in Barcelona had arrived, Redmond had already undergone eight operations due to previous injuries throughout his career.

Despite all of Redmond's injuries and operations, the British runner was in fine form and was considered one of the favorites in the 400m men's event in the Barcelona Olympics. In the first round of the 400m event, Redmond finished with the fastest time and would go on to win the quarter-final race with ease.

Things were looking good for Redmond; he just had the semi-finals left in his way before reaching the men's 400m final, but then tragedy struck. Redmond took his mark for the semi-final and started off like a flash as the gun went off to signal the race. Redmond started the race fantastically, and it looked like he was going to win the semi-final for sure, but then he heard a pop! Redmond knew at that moment his 1992 Olympics run was over. He had torn his hamstring just 250m from the finish line. Redmond was gutted. He was devastated; he worked his entire life to get to this point only to be brought to a cruel halt due to a very unfortunate injury. Redmond began to hobble and fell to the ground in pain, frustration, and disappointment.

What happened next was unbelievable. It was beautiful. A moment that will eternally live on in Olympic history. At the moment that stretcher-bearers came to the British international's aid, Redmond decided that he wanted to finish the race even though the race was over. Redmond got up and began to hobble along the track to the finish line. To the surprise of everyone including Redmond, Derek's father Jim Redmond soon joined his son by swiveling his way past security, to help his son finish the race. Derek leaned on Jim's shoulder, and they slowly marched to the finish line and as father and son crossed the 400m mark where they were met by a standing ovation of 65,000 fans (along with millions of other television spectators with not a dry eye in sight.

Chapter 15: Michael Jordan

Taking "The Shot" in 1989

Michael Jordan is without a doubt the biggest superstar the NBA has known and the first name everybody thinks of when you mention the sport of basketball. Moments like "The Shot" in 1989 are just one of the countless moments that have defined Jordan's legendary career and what signals his greatest of all time (GOAT) status in basketball.

In 1989, Michael Jordan knocked out the Cleveland Cavaliers with a buzzer-beater shot that went down in history as being known as "The Shot" throughout the world, particularly in Cleveland. It is a moment in the sport that will live infinitely in time, especially to the agony of Cleveland Cavaliers and the pure bliss of Chicago Bulls fans who would relive "The Shot" repeatedly as it has been replayed on televisions thousands of times over, and to this day is being replayed on highlight reels and iconic sporting moments. "The Shot" may have only been one basket, but it turned out to play a vital role in the future of the Chicago Bulls, and it is often considered the catalyst of Chicago's dominance of the NBA in the 1990s.

Jordan and the Bulls were to face one of the greatest young teams in NBA history in the form of the Cavaliers. The Cleveland franchise boosted a vast array of talent, including Ron Harper, Mark Price, Larry Nance, John Williams, and Brad Daughtery. Not only was this Cleveland team overflowing with talent, but they were under the influence of one of the NBA's greatest coaches Lenny Wilkens. They were no easy side to face, not even for a Bulls team that had Michael Jordan as a secret weapon.

Under Lenny Wilkens, the Cavaliers achieved a franchise season-best with a record of 57-25, which was 15 games better than their previous season. Cleveland was considered the favorite to bring home the 1988– 1989 NBA title but hit a roadblock when facing Michael Jordan and the Bulls (NBA, 2021).

It was a five-game series between the Bulls and the Cavaliers, and the Bulls had gained home-court advantage from winning the opening game of the series 95-88. The Bulls had the opportunity to close out the set in Chicago but were defeated by Cleveland 108 - 105 in the fourth game of the series, which meant the deciding game would be played in Cleveland.

It all came down to the wire in the final game of the series, and in the closing seconds of the game, Michael Jordan did what he does best—he produced magic! Jordan had the ball with the final seconds ticking down. Jordan from the right side dribbled with absolute grace towards the net and leaped for a jump shot in the circle. Cleveland's best defender, Craig Ehlo attempted to block the shot, but Jordan defied gravity by seemingly floating in the air until Ehlo had descended from his jump, and then Jordan released "The Shot." The shot was good, the Bulls won at the buzzer, and the rest is history.

Chapter 16: Federer vs. Nadal in the 2008 Wimbledon Final

The 2008 Wimbledon final saw two goliaths of the tennis world, Roger Federer and Rafael Nadal, battle it out in one of the most iconic and nail-biting finals in Wimbledon and tennis history. It was no secret that the Swiss Federer and Spanish Nadal had, and still have, a long-standing rivalry, arguably the fiercest rivalry in tennis and sports history, and thus the winner of the 2008 Wimbledon final would secure bragging rights as to who would be the best tennis player in the world. The pair had a combined 14 Grand Slam titles out of the previous 16 Grand Slams prior to the 2008 Wimbledon final.

The 2008 Wimbledon final would signal the third consecutive final at Wimbledon between the Swiss and Spaniard, while Federer had won the previous two meetings in the previous two years in Wimbledon, he had also won the tournament the previous five years, thus signaling he was the king of the grass. On the other hand, Nadal was no walkover and had proven he was the king of clay as he had just won his fourth French Open in four consecutive tournaments, having beaten Federer in the pair's third consecutive encounter in France (Price, 2009). Nadal wanted to win the French Open and Wimbledon double. This is extremely rare as it requires a player to quickly transition from a slower clay court to a faster grass court in only a month (Price, 2009).

The 2008 Wimbledon final commenced, and the Spaniard drew first blood by winning the first two sets 6-4 and 6-4, but Nadal's momentum was interrupted as rain forced play to stop. When play continued, Federer came back with an answer of his own, winning the third set 7-6. The fourth set remained tense throughout, eventually ending with a tiebreak. The 2008 Wimbledon final tiebreak is considered the greatest ever played. The scoreboard was now reading 5-2 in favor of Nadal, and he had the opportunity to put the match to rest with his next two serves, but Nadal's worst nightmare would come to fruition. He double faulted and then lost his grip on the match even more by seeing his backhand netted, which brought the tiebreak back on serve.

Nadal was able to rescue a set point and secured his first championship point; however, the Spaniard failed to return Federer's serve. The score was now 7-7, and Nadal won another championship point by hitting an unbelievable forehand down the line past Federer. Now it was Nadal's turn to serve, but Federer answered with a remarkable backhand of his own that would keep the game alive. The two best shots of the final happened straight after one another. Another forehand winner from Federer brought about set point at 8-7, which he duly took. However, the final took another turn and a second rain delay commenced for 30 minutes.

Both tennis legends returned to the court to find that the court and darkness started to set in, so much so that it threatened to delay the game until the following day. However, the match continued, and during the deciding set, Federer was just two points from winning his sixth Wimbledon title, but Nadal was resilient and held on and finally broke Federer's serve after an astounding 15 games of the final set. Nadal had won the set 9-7 in the 16th game of the set to claim his first Wimbledon, his fifth Grand Slam, and join the Wimbledon-French Open double exclusive club. The match lasted 4 hours and 48 minutes, which was the longest singles final at Wimbledon at the time until that record was broken in 2019 (Price, 2009).

Chapter 17: Usain Bolt at the 2008 Beijing Olympic Games

Usain Bolt is without a doubt the greatest sprinter in history, and it would be an extremely long search before you find someone to disagree with that statement. The Jamaican is superhuman. His speed is mind-boggling, it's hard to comprehend, and it is difficult to even imagine anyone faster than Bolt in the future. The beginning of Bolt's dominance in the world of running began in the 2008 Beijing Olympic games. He expected to be the star of the tournament, and the young Jamaican superstar delivered with flying colors without letting the pressure phase him one bit. He is a top athlete, and as a top athlete, he thrives on pressure. The 2008 Beijing Olympics was Bolt's debut Olympics, and he bossed the world's greatest sporting competition from start to finish.

Bolt was set to compete in two events at the Beijing Olympics. These were the 100m and 200m events, which are arguably two of the most anticipated events of any Olympics, but with Bolt competing in them, the popularity of these events is even more highly anticipated. Bolt came into the Olympics as the fastest man in history as he broke the 100m world record in New York just months before the 2008 Olympics with a time of 9.72 seconds, beating the previous record of 9.74 seconds held by Asaffa Powell (Gallagher, 2008).

In June 2008, Bolt proved that he was not just a 100m sprinter but also a 200m runner and broke the national record with a time of 19.67 seconds in Greece just weeks before the Olympics.

Thus, although this was Bolt's first Olympics, he was still the favorite by some distance to win the gold in both the 100m and 200m events in Beijing despite his inexperience compared to the other athletes. Legendary Olympian Michael Johnson personally believed that Bolt's lack of experience would not work against him as he was simply too talented; however, others were more skeptical than Johnson and did believe that Bolt's inexperience in the Olympics may play against him. Bolt's journey to the 100m final went smoothly, and he easily managed to brush aside the competition recording times of 9.92 seconds to qualify and then 9.85 seconds in both the quarter-finals and semi-finals (Gallagher, 2008).

Next up was the 100m men's final race, and the world was waiting to see just what Usain Bolt was made of. Bolt was hungry for the win and ran the greatest race anybody had ever run in the history of the 100m event at the time. Bolt zoomed past his opposition and ran like he had rockets in his shoes by easily winning the 100m gold in Beijing. He won his first taste of Olympic gold and set a new world record of 9.69 seconds, smashing the current world record of 9.72 seconds that the Jamaican himself had set just a few months before the 2008 Olympics.

What was so iconic about the 100m men's final in Beijing was that Bolt slowed down his pace near the finish line to celebrate before the race was even over and his shoelace was even untied! Bolt's coach and a team of analysts predicted that if Bolt had not slowed down to celebrate, he could have potentially run the race in 9.55 seconds (Gallagher, 2008). Absolutely astonishing. Bolt had stunned the globe and instantly became a household name. Bolt had carved his name in history and the world had found its new king of the 100m.

Bolt wasn't done yet as he still had his eyes set on the 200m men's final, an event that he had been training on and did not come as naturally to him as the 100m. Bolt wanted to emulate Carl Lewis's 100m and 200m gold medal double in the 1986 Olympics, but he also had his eye on breaking Michael Johnson's 200m record set in the 1996 Olympics. Michael Johnson was an admirer of the Jamaican and felt that Bolt would win the 200m men's final in Beijing, but he also felt that Bolt wouldn't break his 19.32 second 200m record that he set in 1996.

The day of the men's 200m final had arrived, and to the surprise of nobody, Bolt won his second gold of the Olympics. A cherry was added on top of Bolt's 200m win when he broke Michael Johnson's 19.32 seconds 200m world record when Bolt finished with a time of 19.30 seconds, despite running against a 0.9 m/s headwind (Gallagher, 2008). Bolt had just broken the men's 100m and 200m world records in a matter of days and in the same Olympics—a momentous feat. He had also become the first athlete to ever achieve this since the introduction of electronic timing. The Jamaican was a machine, and he was not done yet.

Bolt would participate just two days later in the 400m relays for Team Jamaica to help Jamaica win the gold and add yet another gold medal to Bolt's unthinkably spectacular 2008 Olympic medal heist from the track. Bolt at the 2008 Beijing Olympics was simply remarkable and ensured that his name will live within the public's consciousness for centuries to come.

Chapter 18: Michael Phelps Breaking Gold Medal Record in 2008

Has there ever been a greater performance at a single sporting event/tournament in history than Michael Phelps' gold medal total eight gold medal heist at the 2008 Beijing Olympics? I don't think so, and it will be a long search to even find a performance that comes close to winning eight Olympic gold medals in one single Olympics like Phelps did on the world's biggest sporting stage.

To win four gold medals at one Olympics seems nearly impossible, but to win eight gold medals in one Olympics sounds like a lie you tell your buddies on the school playground to sound macho. The mere thought of it sounds insane. It sounds like a movie script. It sounds like a hoax. However, let me assure you this is no hoax since this was achieved by one of the greatest athletes of all time and his name was Michael Phelps—the greatest Olympian of all time.

This is how the epic tale of Michael Phelps 2008 Beijing Olympics rolled out. Phelps started with a bang in Beijing by winning his first gold medal in the 400m individual medley. He didn't only win his first medal at this Olympic Games, but he also obliterated the previous world record he held in this event by just under two seconds! Phelps followed up on his outrageously impressive start to the 2008 Olympics by winning his second gold medal by swimming in the first leg of the 4 x 100m freestyle relay for Team USA. Phelps finished his first leg of the relay with a staggering time of 47.51 seconds, which was a new American record.

Phelps won his third gold medal in the 200m freestyle and broke yet another world record (held by him already) by almost an entire second. This gold medal also marked his ninth Olympic gold medal in total, joining the ranks of fellow Olympians Mark Spitz, Larisa Latynina, Carl Lewis, and Paavo Nurmi, who are the only other Olympians to have achieved this feat at the time.

Next was the 200m Butterfly in which Phelps set an impressive time of 1:52.03 minutes, securing his fourth Olympic gold medal in Beijing and his 10th total Olympic gold, making him the most decorated gold medalist in modern Olympic history. He won the 200m butterfly despite having his goggles fill up with water, preventing the Olympian from seeing anything for approximately 100m of the 200m race. This gold medal also meant that Phelps became the first swimmer to successfully defend his butterfly gold medal title in two consecutive Olympics (Associated Press, 2008).

Just an hour after Phelps' 200m butterfly gold medal win, he would go on to secure his fifth gold medal in Beijing as he swam the lead-off leg for Team USA in the

4 x 200m freestyle relay. Team USA finished the relay with an astounding time of 6:58.56 minutes, setting a new world record and becoming the first relay team to break the seven-minute mark in the 4 x 200m freestyle relay.

In Phelps' next event, he swam the 200m individual medley and set his sixth world record of the 2008 Beijing Olympics with a time of 1:54.23 to achieve his sixth medal of these Olympics and 12th overall. Although Phelps would go on to win his seventh medal in his next event, the 100m butterfly, it would be his closest call yet. Phelps won the race, won his seventh gold medal in Beijing, and set a new Olympic record with a time of 50.58 seconds. This was not without controversy as with in-depth analysis, it was found Phelps only won the race by the nearest of margins. Thorough analysis showed that Phelps won with a 10-thousandth of a second separating Phelps and second place Milorad Cavic. However, the seventh medal for Phelps was secured, and he had tied the record for seven gold medals in one single Olympics, which had only been done before by legendary swimmer Mark Spitz in the 1972 Olympic games. The 100m butterfly also marked his fifth individual gold medal at the Olympics, which meant he had tied the record with Eric Heiden who achieved this feat in the 1980 Winter Olympics and Vitaly Scherbo who did the same in the 1992 Summer Olympics.

However, on August 17, 2008, Phelps would no longer share the record with Mark Spitz of seven Olympic gold medals at a single Olympics, as he broke it by becoming the first Olympian in history to win eight gold medals. Phelps won his record eighth Olympic gold medal in Beijing and 14th overall in the 4 x 100m medley relay. Phelps and Team USA set another world record, finishing with a time of 3:29.34 minutes, an astonishing 1.34 seconds faster than the previous record set by Team USA. One thing is for certain the Beijing Olympic games will always be remembered as the Michael Phelps Olympics, the Olympics where one man was literally unstoppable.

Chapter 19: Simone Biles Becoming the Most Decorated Gymnast of All-Time

Simone Biles is a once-in-a-lifetime athlete. She is the greatest gymnast the world has ever seen, and she proved that in 2019 when she became the most decorated gymnast of all time, and she did that all at the tender age of 22. It is truly remarkable. Biles added to her already incredible trophy cabinet with five more world gymnastics medals in the 2019 Stuttgart World Gymnastics Championships.

The seemingly superhuman Biles took home five of the six gold medals up for grabs in Stuttgart, as she won gold in the team competition, the all-around, the floor, beam, and the vault events in Germany. The only gold medal that eluded her in Stuttgart was the uneven bars in which the American gymnast ranked fifth (Wamsley, 2019). These five medals meant that Biles would overtake the previous record holder, the legendary Russian gymnast, Svetlana Khorkina (20 medals), thus becoming the most decorated female gymnast in the history of the sport with 21 world medals.

During the team final event, Biles would help lead team USA to their fifth consecutive gold medal title. Biles contributed to the gold medal by achieving unfathomably impressive scores with a 15.400 on vault, 14.600 on uneven bars, 14.443 on the balance beam, and 15.333 on floor exercise (Barnas, 2016). These scores would also mean that Biles managed to set the highest scores on the day for the balance beam, vault, and floor exercises. Thus, Biles had won her first of five medals in Stuttgart with relative ease.

Next was the all-round final where Biles would win her second of five gold medals in Germany, achieving a score of 58.999. This also meant that Biles would set a record of being a mammoth 2.1 points ahead of second place Chinese gymnast Tang Xijing. Unbelievably, Biles would go on to set the highest scores of the day again on vault, floor exercise, and the balance beam!

Biles had cleaned up, but she was not done. Next on her hit list was the gold medal for the vault. Once again, Biles dominated and won her third of five gold medals in Germany after beating Great Britain's Ellie Downie. However, the next event was the uneven bars where Biles did not fare as well as the rest of her extraordinary performance, finishing fifth with a score of 14.700.

Despite finishing fifth in her most recent event and already winning three gold medals thus far in Germany, she was not done yet. The next event was the balance beam, in which Biles narrowly beat the reigning balance beam champion of the time Liu Tingting and her Chinese compatriot Li Shija by just 0.6 points to win her fourth gold medal in Stuttgart (Barnas,2016). This medal meant that Biles had now achieved a total of 24 medals in her illustrious career and was now the sole record holder for the most medals by a gymnast. This was significant as she surpassed male gymnast Vitaly Sherbero as the leading medal holder as a gymnast regardless of gender.

Biles would win her fifth and final gold medal of the 2019 World Championships in Stuttgart in the floor exercise event by scoring a highly impressive score of 15.133. Biles's score in the floor exercise event meant she would finish with exactly one point more than second place Lee, securing her 25th gymnastics medal. Biles' momentous achievement of achieving five gold medals in one World Championship is almost unthinkable and it is a performance that will go down in history as one of, if not the greatest, performances at a single gymnastics tournament.

Chapter 20: Emma Raducanu

Winning the US Open

When Emma Raducanu won the 2021 US Open, it was probably the biggest surprise in tennis history. Raducanu won at the tender age of just 18, which is astonishing, but that is not what makes her maiden Grand Slam win so impressive. There were so many factors playing against her. There have been many sporting prodigies in sports history that have pulled off fantastic title wins at such a young age, but generally, these prodigies are already household names, and the world was already made aware of their talents. For example, athletes such as Boris Becker, Tiger Woods, Serena Williams, Mike Tyson, and Kylian Mbappe all achieved momentous achievements at a very young age, and even if they were from different sports, they were all household names expected to achieve great things. However, this was not the case with Raducanu, who was a virtual unknown with very little professional tennis experience or tennis tournament success. Thus, when the half-Romanian and half-Chinese British migrant won the 2021 US Open, it was a massive "Did that just happen?" moment.

Despite Raducanu's age and lack of experience, she had also just finished high school a couple of months before winning one of tennis's biggest prizes. On top of that, before 2021, Raducanu had only ever played in front of a crowd of little more than 100 people (Today, 2021). Furthermore, Raducanu was not in the main draw of the 2021 US Open and had to play three matches just to enter the competition as a qualifier. In the qualifying rounds, Raducanu won against Mariam Bolvadxe, Bibiane Schoofs, and Mayar Sherif to ensure her spot in the main draw. Thus, Raducanu entered the 2021 US Open as a qualifier and was ranked as only the 150th best female tennis player in the world (Ankle, 2021). Therefore, you can understand why the British migrant was not favored at all at the US Open. Everyone assumed that Raducanu would bow out after the first round, and if she was lucky, she would play two rounds. However, that was as far from a chance as the world had given this virtual unknown.

Raducanu proved the world wrong and quickly swept through her opponents at the 2019 US Open and each win gave the 18-year-old greater confidence, which was evident in her performances that seemed to get better and better with each match. On her road to the final, the Brit beat Stefanie Vögele, Zhang Shuai, Sara Sorribes Tormo, Shelby Rogers, Belinda Bencic, and Maria Sakkari. What is even more bewildering is that Raducanu did not drop a single set. This unbelievable journey meant that the 18-year-old prodigy would go on to break countless records. Raducanu jumped over 100 ranking places on her road to the final and was in the top 25 best female tennis stars in the world and the number 1 ranked female British tennis player. She would also make history by becoming the first qualifier to reach the finals of a Grand Slam in the entirety of the

Open era, as well as becoming the youngest finalist at any grand slam since Maria Sharapova in 2005! To top that off, the 18-year-old would join the elusive club of being only one of five tennis players to reach the semi-final of the US Open during a debut tournament. If those records were not impressive enough, Raducanu became the first female British US Open finalist in 53 years, this feat was last achieved by Virginia Wade (Pa Sport Staff, 2021).

Raducanu had one more hurdle to overcome: the 19-year-old Canadian tennis superstar Leyla Fernandez, who was the favorite of the two to bring home the 2021 US Open. It would also mark the first all-teenage female final in the US Open in 22 years with the last one being the 1999 US Open featuring Serena Williams vs. Martina Hingis. Although Fernandez was the favorite to win the US Open, she was no match for Raducanu who swept her away without dropping a set, the first female winner to do so at a US Open final since Serena Williams in 2014. The 18-year-old won 6-4 and 6-3 in the final (Syed, 2021). Her win also signaled that she is the first qualifier to win a Grand Slam in the Open era. She also is only one of two female tennis stars to win the US Open in a debut tournament. Raducanu rejoiced in victory and transitioned from being a virtually unknown tennis player to becoming the champion of the 2021 US Open.

Conclusion

One of the most widely discussed topics in sports is which sporting moment is the greatest moment in history? This is almost impossible to conclusively say since it is so subjective that someone may say Michael Phelps at the 2008 Olympics, while another might say it was Super Bowl LI in 2017. However, one thing is for sure and that is each one of these iconic and memorable moments can be argued to take top spot as the greatest sporting moment of all time. Each moment is filled with awe-inspiring, almost unbelievable narratives that make you wonder if fact sometimes really is stranger than fiction.

Whether the greatest moment was when the Springboks won the 1995 Rugby World Cup and laid the foundation of a democratic South Africa or the absolute masterclass of Jesse Owens in Berlin, proving everybody wrong, does not matter as both moments were magical. Both will live on in history and both will be remembered with the same level of fondness, legacy, and significance. Moments like these are why sports are beautiful. Moments like these provide clarity as to why billions of people are obsessed with sports and follow these moments so closely. They inspire. They motivate. They give people hope and the ambition to dream big. They let the world know that anything is possible and that magic truly does exist.

Moments like Derek Redmond finishing the 400m

semi-final with the help of his father at the 1992 Olympics are moments of beauty, not because of the performance, but because of what it represented and the message it sent out. When Leicester City defied 5000/1 odds to win the English Premier League, it meant that anything is possible if you are willing to fight for it and dream big. Moments such as Emma Raducanu miraculously winning the US Open as an unknown being ranked 150th in the world inspired the world with a message of never let someone else tell you what you can and cannot do. Never underestimate the underdog. The awe-inspiring comeback of Super Bowl LI in 2017 is a moment that inspires us to never give up no matter how bad things seem. The Red Sox winning the World Series for the first time in 86 years taught us that there is always light at the end of the tunnel no matter how long that tunnel is.

You could go through each one of these moments and find inspiring and motivating life lessons that we could all learn from. Each moment is so unique and so impactful leaving behind a legacy that will never be forgotten, and that is why these are the *20 Greatest Sporting Moments of All-Time.*

References

Ankel, S. (2021, September 12). *Emma Raducanu, whose stunning victory at the US Open earned her $2.5 million, said her initial goal was to win enough prize money to replace her lost AirPods.* Insider. https://www.insider.com/emma-raducanus-goal-before-us-open-win-was-replace-airpods-2021-9

Associated Press. (2008, August 16). *Phenomenal Phelps wins 7th gold by 0.01 seconds to tie Spitz. ESPN.* *https://www.espn.com/olympics/summer08/swimming/news/story?id=3537831*

Barnas, J.A. (2016, August 14). *Biles becomes most decorated U.S. gymnast with Olympic vault gold.* USA Gymnastics. https://usagym.org/pages/post.html?PostID=19143&prog=

Casiano, L. (2020, February 11). *Buster Douglas KO's Mike Tyson in one of the sports world's biggest upsets: This Day in History.* Fox News. https://www.foxnews.com/sports/buster-douglas-kos-mike-tyson-sports-worlds-biggest-upsets-this-day-in-history

Classic Boxing Matches. (2016, October 1). *"The Rumble in the Jungle" Muhammad Ali vs George Foreman 30.10.1974.* YouTube. https://www.youtube.com/watch?v=ElWMImS6K78

Crean, T. (2021, August 30). *The Rumble in the Jungle was a Fair Fight because both Muhammad Ali and George Foreman's Camps Paid off the Ref.* Sports Casting. https://www.sportscasting.com/rumble-in-the-jungle-fair-fight-because-both-muhammad-ali-george-foremans-camps-paid-off-ref/

Glendenning, B. (2005, May 25). *Liverpool 3 - 3 AC Milan*. The Guardian. https://www.theguardian.com/football/2005/may/25/minutebyminute.championsleague

Hughes, I. (2004, May 15). *Arsenal the Invincibles*. BBC Sport. http://news.bbc.co.uk/sport2/hi/football/teams/a/arsenal/3713537.stm

Jones, J. (2018, December 12). *Buster Douglas reveals how death of mum just weeks before Mike Tyson fight inspired him into shocking boxing world*. The Sun. https://www.thesun.co.uk/sport/7958290/buster-douglas-death-mum-mike-tyson-fight-boxing/

Cleary, M., & Donegan, L. (1995, 26 June). *Afrikaans arrogance sours Springboks' taste of victory*. The Guardian. https://www.theguardian.com/sport/1995/jun/26/rugbyworldcup2003.rugbyunion1

Gallagher, B. (2008, August 6). *Beijing Olympics: Usain Bolt set to run in both the 100 and 200 meters*. Telegraph. https://web.archive.org/web/20080817225244/http://www.telegraph.co.uk/sport/othersports/olympics/2506738/2008-Beijing-Olympics-Usain-Bolt-

set-to-run-in-both-the-100-and-200-metres---
Olympics.html

Kory, M. (2014, October 27). *Let's relive the Red Sox
2004 World Series: 86 years of frustration ends in
Game 4*. Over the Monster.
https://www.overthemonster.com/2014/10/27/70
77057/red-sox-world-series-2004-derek-lowe-trot-
nixon

McNulty, P. (2012, May 13). Man City 3-2 QPR. *BBC
Sport.*
https://www.bbc.com/sport/football/17973148.

NBA (2021, September 14). *Top Moments: Michael
Jordan hits "The Shot", breaks Cavs' hearts.*
Www.nba.com.
https://www.nba.com/news/history-top-
moments-jordan-shot-cavaliers-1989

New England Patriots. (2017, February 5). *Super
Bowl LI*. New England Patriots.
https://www.patriots.com/press-room/super-
bowl-li

Ohio State University. (2020). *1936 Olympics | Jesse
Owens: A Lasting Legend*. OSU.EDU.
https://library.osu.edu/site/jesseowens/1936-
olympics/

Pa Sport Staff. (2021, September 12). *Focus on 1968:
The last time a British woman won US Open
before Emma Raducanu*. Independent.
https://www.independent.co.uk/sport/tennis/em
ma-raducanu-martin-luther-king-jr-british-focus-
united-b1918539.html

Patterson, C. (2019, April 15). 2019 Masters: All the
ways Tiger Woods made history in winning his fifth

green jacket. CBS Sports.
https://www.cbssports.com/golf/news/2019-masters-all-the-ways-tiger-woods-made-history-in-winning-his-fifth-green-jacket/

Price, S.L. (2009, May 14). *How Nadal humbled Federer*. Sports Illustrated.
https://www.si.com/more-sports/2009/05/14/federer-nadal

Ronay, B. (2016, May 2). *The Leicester Supremacy – a triumph that was never supposed to happen.* The Guardian.
https://www.theguardian.com/football/blog/2016/may/02/leicester-city-champions-premier-league

Rothman, L. (2015, June 24). *See Photos from South Africa's Monumental Rugby World Cup Victory.* Time.com; Time. https://time.com/3913350/1995-rugby-world-cup/

Runyon, J. (2014, April 5). *Impossible Case Study: Sir Roger Bannister and The Four-Minute Mile | IMPOSSIBLE* ®. Https://Impossiblehq.com/.
https://impossiblehq.com/impossible-case-study-sir-roger-bannister/#:~:text=Sir%20Roger%20Bannister%20was%20the%20first%20man%20to

Syed, Y. (2021, September 24). *What Emma Raducanu said before championship point vs Leylah Fernandez at US Open.* Express.co.uk.
https://www.express.co.uk/sport/tennis/1496220/Emma-Raducanu-Leylah-Fernandez-US-Open-British-tennis-news-WTA-Tour

Today. (2021, September 13). *Emma Raducanu talks about her history-making tennis win at US Open.*

TODAY.com.
https://www.today.com/video/emma-raducanu-
talks-about-her-history-making-tennis-win-at-us-
open-120739397689

Vasilogambros, M. (2016, May 2). *Leicester City, the
Unlikeliest of Winners*. The Atlantic.
https://www.theatlantic.com/entertainment/archi
ve/2016/05/leicester-city-premier-
league/480918/

Wamsley, L. (2019, October 13). *Simone Biles
Becomes the Most Decorated Gymnast In World
Championship History*. Houston Public Media.
https://www.npr.org/2019/10/13/769896721/sim
one-biles-becomes-the-most-decorated-gymnast-
in-world-championship-history

Weinburg, R. (2004, May 25). *94: Derek and dad
finish Olympic 400 together*. ESPN.
https://www.espn.com/espn/espn25/story?page=
moments/94

Westin, D. (2019, April 14). *Tiger Woods wins 2019
Masters Tournament*. Www.augusta.com.
https://www.augusta.com/masters/story/news/20
19-04-14/tiger-woods-wins-2019-masters-
tournament

Wikipedia. (2021k, September 27). *Emma Raducanu*.
Wikipedia.
https://en.wikipedia.org/wiki/Emma_Raducanu#
Grand_Slam_tournament_finals

Printed in Great Britain
by Amazon